2ⁿᵈ Edition

IRISH BLESSINGS

Over 100 Irish Blessings in 8 Categories

Jean LeGrand

Irish Heritage books from Jean LeGrand:

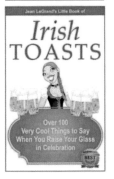

A SURPRISE GIFT

To say "Thanks" for buying this book, I would like to give you a FREE COPY of *Irish Fairy Tales.*

If you're of Irish descent or if you like Irish culture or if you like reading great stories, you're going to want this book of incredible Irish tales.

Just go enter this web address: goo.gl/82Grjh on your browser and when you see the "Yes, I Want a Free Book" button, click it.

Enjoy … it's just my way of saying, "Thanks!" for buying *Irish Blessings.*

TABLE OF CONTENTS

DEDICATION

For my nieces, Kaela and Braelyn,
two blessings of the highest degree.

INTRODUCTION

Passed down without attributing their original authors and quoted in all different settings from pub crawls to christenings, Irish blessings are recognized as positive affirmations of support and good will. They are appropriate at any number of life celebrations from weddings to funerals to commencement ceremonies.

The Irish blessing (and cursing tradition) is credited the Druids and Filidh; gaining strength with the Celt's deeply held belief in the inherent power of the spoken word.

The Irish Blessings we know today, evolved from the farming culture of early Ireland. These hard-working people with little wealth, found comfort in the concept of the heavenly reward of their God bestowing good fortune and prosperity on the good-hearted. So depending on mutual support, the Irish farming families celebrated honesty and hospitality.

One of the most quoted traditional Irish Blessings is known as "A Blessing from St. Patrick":

May the road rise to meet you,
May the wind be always at your back,
May the sun shine warm upon your face,
May the rains fall soft upon your fields,
And, until we meet again,
May God hold you in the hollow of His hand.

Although often attributed to St. Patrick, it is highly unlikely that he actually said this ... but that does not distract from the blessing's positive and uplifting message.

When reading through these well-turned phrases, it is not unusual for people to find one or two blessings that seem to hold a special message them. If you find yourself in that position, take a moment to write it/them down. If you do so, legend says that within a fortnight (2 weeks) you will find a use for that blessing to offer much needed comfort and hope to yourself, a family member, or a friend in need.

"The hands are there for friendship, the heart is there for love. For loyalty throughout the year, the crown is raised above."

61 IRISH BLESSINGS

May you always have walls for the winds,
a roof for the rain, tea beside the fire,
laughter to cheer you, those you love near you,
and all your heart might desire.

For each petal on the shamrock.
This brings a wish your way
Good health, good luck, and
happiness
For today and every day.

May you have warm words on a cold evening,
a full moon on a dark night,
and the road downhill all the way to your door.

May God give you…
For every storm, a rainbow,
For every tear, a smile,
For every care, a promise,
And a blessing in each trial.
For every problem life sends,
A faithful friend to share,
For every sigh, a sweet song,
And an answer for each prayer.

May you have love that never ends,
lots of money, and lots of friends.
Health be yours, whatever you do,
and may God send many blessings to you!

May your feet never sweat,
your neighbor give you ne're a treat.
When flowers bloom, I hope you'll not sneeze,
and may you always have someone to squeeze!

May the sun shine, all day long,
everything go right,
and nothing wrong.
May those you love
bring love back to you,
and may all the wishes you wish
come true!

I-rish you a very nice place to live,
I-rish God's greatest gifts he'll give.
I-rish you health, and wealth, and more--
I-rish your smilin' face were at my door!

May you have:
A world of wishes at your command.
God and his angels close to hand.
Friends and family their love impart,
and Irish blessings in your heart!

May you always walk in sunshine.
May you never want for more.
May Irish angels rest their wings right beside your door.

May God grant you many years to live,
For sure he must be knowing.
The earth has angels all too few.
And heaven is overflowing.

May good luck be your friend
In whatever you do.
And may trouble be always
A stranger to you.

May God grant you always...
A sunbeam to warm you,
A moonbeam to charm you,
A sheltering angel, so nothing can harm you.

May the embers from the open hearth warm your hands,
May the sun's rays from the Irish sky warm your face,
May the children's bright smiles warm your heart,
May the everlasting love I give you warm your soul.

May your thoughts be as glad as the shamrocks,
May your heart be as light as a song,
May each day bring you bright, happy hours,
That stay with you all the year long.

Leprechauns, castles, good luck and laughter.
Lullabies, dreams and love ever after.
A thousand welcomes when anyone comes...
That's the Irish for You!

Whenever there is happiness
Hope you'll be there too,
Wherever there are friendly smiles
Hope they'll smile on you,
Whenever there is sunshine,
Hope it shine especially for you to make each day
for you as bright as it can be

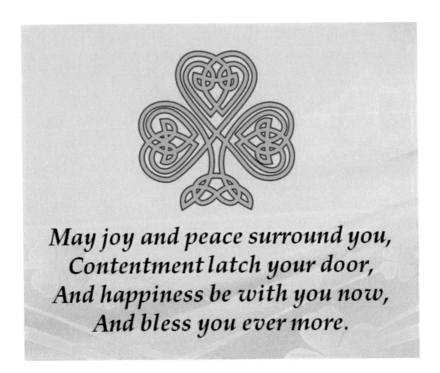

May joy and peace surround you,
Contentment latch your door,
And happiness be with you now,
And bless you ever more.

May the good saints protect you,
And bless you today.
And may troubles ignore you,
Each step of the way.

May the saint protect ye-
An' sorrow neglect ye,
An' bad luck to the one
That doesn't respect ye
t' all that belong to ye,
And long life t' yer honor-
That's the end of my song t' ye!

These things, I warmly wish for you-
Someone to love, some work to do,
A bit of o' sun, a bit o' cheer.
And a guardian angel always near.

.

May your troubles be less,
And your blessing be more.
And nothing but happiness,
Come through your door.

May brooks and trees and
singing hills
Join in the chorus too,
And every gentle wind that blows
Send happiness to you.

Lucky stars above you,
Sunshine on your way,
Many friends to love you,
Joy in work and play-
Laughter to outweigh each care,
In your heart, a song-
And gladness waiting everywhere
All your whole life long!

When the first light of sun-
Bless you.
When the long day is done-
Bless you.
In your smiles and your tears-
Bless you.
Through each day of your years-
Bless you.

May the raindrops fall lightly on your brow.
May the soft winds freshen your spirit.
May the sunshine brighten your heart
May the burdens of the day rest lightly upon you.
And may God enfold you in the mantle of His love.

He who loses money, loses much;
He who loses a friend, loses more;
He who loses faith, loses all.

May you enjoy the four greatest blessings:
Honest work to occupy you.
A hearty appetite to sustain you.
A good woman to love you.
And a wink from the God above.

*May the wings of the butterfly
kiss the sun.
And find your shoulder to light on.
To bring you luck, happiness
and riches.
Today, tomorrow and beyond.*

May you live a long life
Full of gladness and health,
With a pocket full of gold
As the least of your wealth.
May the dreams you hold dearest,
Be those which come true,
The kindness you spread,
Keep returning to you.

May the friendships you make,
Be those which endure,
And all of your grey clouds
Be small ones for sure.
And trusting in Him
To Whom we all pray,
May a song fill your heart,
Every step of the way.

Here's to health, peace and prosperity.
May the flower of love
never be nipped by the frost of disappointment,
nor shadow of grief fall among your family and friends.

May your troubles be less,
And your blessing be more.
And nothing but happiness,
Come through your door.

May the road rise up to meet you.
May the wind always be
at your back.
May the sun shine warm
upon your face,
and rains fall soft upon your fields.
And until we meet again,
May God hold you in
the palm of His hand.

May love and laughter light your days,
and warm your heart and home.
May good and faithful friends be yours,
wherever you may roam.
May peace and plenty bless your world
with joy that long endures.
May all life's passing seasons
bring the best to you and yours!

Wishing you always...
Walls for the wind,
A roof for the rain
And tea beside the fire.
Laughter to cheer you,
Those you love near you,
And all that your heart may desire

Deep peace of the running waves to you.
Deep peace of the flowing air to you.
Deep peace of the smiling stars to you.
Deep peace of the quiet earth to you.
Deep peace of the watching shepherds to you.
Deep peace of the Son of Peace to you

May the frost never afflict your spuds.
May the leaves of your cabbage always
be free from worms.
May the crows never pick your haystack.
If you inherit a donkey, may she be in foal.
May there always be work for your hands to do.
May your purse always hold a coin or two.
May the sun always shine on your windowpane.
May a rainbow be certain to follow each rain.
May the hand of a friend always be near you.
May God fill your heart with gladness to cheer you.

*May your day be touched
by a bit of Irish luck,
brightened by a song in your heart,
and warmed by the smiles
of the people you love.*

Grant me a sense of humor, Lord,
the saving grace to see a joke,
To win some happiness from life,
And pass it on to other folks.

May the good earth be soft under you
when you rest upon it,
and may it rest easy over you when,
at the last, you lay out under it,
And may it rest so lightly over you
that your soul may be out
from under it quickly,
and up, and off,
And be on its way to God.

Wishing you a rainbow
For sunlight after showers—
Miles and miles of Irish smiles
For golden happy hours—
Shamrocks at your doorway
For luck and laughter too,
And a host of friends that never ends
Each day your whole life through!

May you be poor in misfortune,
Rich in blessings,
Slow to make enemies,
And quick to make friends.
But rich or poor, quick or slow,
May you know nothing but happiness
From this day forward

May you have food and raiment,
A soft pillow for your head,
May you be forty years in heaven
Before the devil knows you're dead.

May you get all your wishes but one,
so that you will always have something to strive for!

Walls for the wind,
And a roof for the rain,
And drinks beside the fire -
Laughter to cheer you
And those you love near you,
And all that your heart may desire!

May the lilt of Irish laughter Lighten every load,
May the mist of Irish magic Shorten every road,
May you taste the sweetest pleasures
That fortune ere bestowed,
And may all your friends remember.
All the favors you are owed.

When the first light of sun-
Bless you
When the long day is done-
Bless you
In your smiles and your tears-
Bless you
Through each day of your years-
Bless you.

May green be the grass you walk on,
May blue be the skies above you,
May pure be the joys
that surround you,
May true be the hearts
that love you.

May the grace of God's protection
And His great love abide
Within your home-within the hearts
Of all who dwell inside.

Like the warmth of the sun
And the light of the day,
May the luck of the Irish
shine bright on your way.

May your heart be light and happy,
May your smile be big and wide,
And may your pockets always have
a coin or two inside!

*May your mornings bring joy
and your evenings bring peace...
May your troubles grow less
as your blessings increase!*

Always remember to forget
The troubles that passed away.
But never forget to remember
The blessings that come each day.

May neighbors respect you,
Trouble neglect you,
The angels protect you,
And heaven accept you.

May you have the hindsight to know where you've been,
The foresight to know where you are going,
And the insight to know when you have gone too far.

May those that love us, love us.
And those that don't love us,
May God turn their hearts.
And if he doesn't turn their hearts,
May he turn their ankles,
So we'll know them by their limping.

May you be in heaven a full half hour
before the devil knows your dead.

If you're enough lucky to be Irish...
You're lucky enough!

May your pockets be heavy —
Your heart be light,
And may good luck pursue you
Each morning and night.

May the luck of the Irish
Lead to happiest heights
And the highway you travel
Be lined with green lights.

May the blessing of light be on you—
light without and light within.
May the blessed sunlight shine on you
and warm your heart
till it glows like a great peat fire.

May you have all the happiness
and luck that life can hold—
And at the end of all your rainbows
may you find a pot of gold.

Cliffs of Slieve League, County Donegal

5 ST. PATRICK'S DAY BLESSINGS

Beannachtaí Na Féile Pádraig (St. Patrick's Day Blessings)

*May the leprechauns be near you,
to spread luck along your way.
And may all the Irish angels, smile
upon you on St. Patrick's Day.*

May the Irish hills caress you.
May her lakes and rivers bless you.
May the luck of the Irish enfold you.
May the blessings of Saint Patrick behold you.

May your blessings outnumber the Shamrocks that grow,
And may trouble avoid you Wherever you go.
Happy St. Patrick's Day!

May the love and protection Saint Patrick can give
Be yours in abundance as long as you live.

May St. Patrick guard you wherever you go,
and guide you in whatever you do--
and may his loving protection be a blessing to you always.

28 ONE LINE BLESSINGS

Like the warmth of the sun and the light of the day,
may the luck of the Irish shine bright on your way.

May the roof over your heads be as well thatched
As those inside are well matched.

*May your neighbors respect you,
Trouble neglect you, The angels
protect you, and heaven accept you.*

May your home always be too small
to hold all your friends.

May I see you grey and
combing your grandchildren's hair.

May you have all the happiness and luck that life can hold;
and at the end of your rainbows May you find a pot of
gold.

A special Irish blessing from the heart of a friend;
"May good fortune be yours; May your joys never end."

May good luck be with you Wherever you go,
And your blessing outnumber the shamrocks that grow

May this home and all therein be blessed with God's love

May the Lord keep you in His hand and
never close His fist too tight.

Wherever you go and whatever you do,
may the luck of the Irish be there with you.

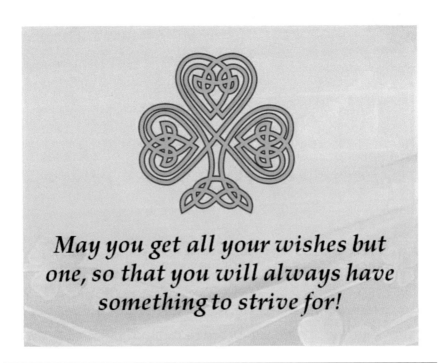

*May you get all your wishes but
one, so that you will always have
something to strive for!*

May your troubles be less and your blessing be more
And nothing but happiness Come through your door

May the most you wish for be the least you get.

If God sends you down a stony path, may he give you
strong shoes.

May you always have a clean shirt, a clear conscience,
and enough coins in your pocket to buy a pint!

If you're enough lucky to be Irish...You're lucky enough!

May you escape the gallows, avoid distress, and be as
healthy as a trout.
God between us and all harm.

May the face of every good news and
the back of every bad news be towards us.

*Peace on your hand and
health to all who shake it.*

Health and long life to you, land without rent to you,
a child every year to you, and death in Old Ireland.

May the saddest day of your future be no worse than
the happiest day of your past.

May misfortune follow you the rest of your life,
and never catch up.

May the roof above you never fall in;
and those gathered beneath it never fall out.

May you always have these blessings: a soft breeze when
summer comes - a warm fireside in winter - and always -
the warm, soft smile of a friend.

May you live as long as you want
and never want as long as you live.

8 BLESSINGS IN GAELIC
(with Translation & Pronunciation)

Gaelic: Go n-eirí an t-ádh leat
(pronounced *Guh nye-ree on taw laht.*)
English: Good luck to you
(Literal: 'That luck may rise with you')

Go n-eírí an bóthar leat

May the road rise with you

Gaelic: Sláinte chugat
(pronounced *Slawn-cheh ch(k)oo-at*
English: Good health to you.

Gaelic: Saol fada agus breac-shláinte chugat
(pronounced *Say-ol faw-dah og-uss brack- hlawn-cheh
ch(k)oo-at)*
English: Long-life and fair health to you.

Gaelic: Go raibh míle maith agat
(pronounced *Guh rev mee-lah maw og-ut)*
English: Many thanks!
(literal: 'That you may have a thousand good things')

Gaelic: Mo sheacht mbeannacht ort
(pronounced *Muh hyawch(k)t mann-ach(k)t urt)*
English: My seven blessings on you!

Sliocht sleachta ar shliocht bhur sleachta.

May there be a generation of children on the children of your children.

Gaelic: Maith thú
(pronounced *Maw hoo)*
English: Good on you

Gaelic: Nár laga Dia thú
(pronounced *Nawr lag-ah Dee-ah hoo)*
English: May God never weaken you

Gaelic: Codladh sámh
(pronounced *Cuh-lah sawve*)
English: Sleep well

Geroid Island, Lough Gur

A WEDDING BLESSING

Happy Is The Bride That Rain Falls On

Happy is the bride that rain falls on
May your mornings bring joy
and your evenings bring peace.
May your troubles grow few as your blessings increase.
May the saddest day of your future
Be no worse than the happiest day of your past.
May your hands be forever clasped in friendship
And your hearts joined forever in love.
Your lives are very special,
God has touched you in many ways.
May his blessings rest upon you
And fill all your coming days.
We swear by peace and love to stand,
Heart to heart and hand to hand.
Hark, O Spirit, and hear us now,
Confirming this our Sacred Vow.

Celtic Wedding Rings

5 CHRISTMAS BLESSINGS

May you be blessed
With the spirit of the season, which is peace,
The gladness of the season, which is hope,
And the heart of the season, which is love.

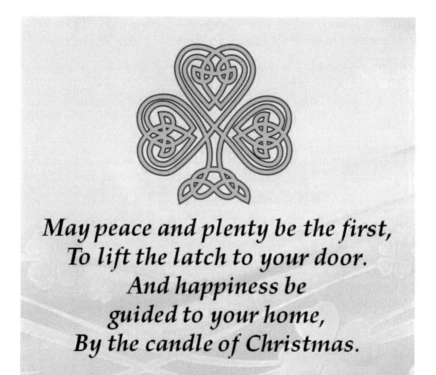

May peace and plenty be the first,
To lift the latch to your door.
And happiness be
guided to your home,
By the candle of Christmas.

May the Blessings of Christmas be with you,
May the Christ Child light your way,
May God's holy angels guide you,
And keep you safe each day.

The light of the Christmas star to you,
The warmth of home and hearth to you,
The cheer and good will of friends to you,
The hope of a childlike heart to you,
The joy of a thousand angels to you,
The love of the Son,
And God's peace to you.

Nollaig faoi shéan is faoi shonas duit.
(A prosperous and happy Christmas to you!)

Doneraile Park and House, County Cork

An EASTER BLESSING

Beannachtaí na Cásca Oraibh
(Easter Blessings)

At the breaking of the Easter dawn
May the Risen Savior bless your home
With grace and peace from above,
With joy and laughter, and with love;
And when night is nigh, and day is done
May He keep you safe from all harm.

Roosky

2 FUNERAL BLESSINGS

Remembered Joy

Don't grieve for me, for now I'm free!
I follow the plan God laid for me.
I saw His face, I heard His call,
I took His hand and left it all...
I could not stay another day,
To love, to laugh, to work or play;
Tasks left undone must stay that way.
And if my parting has left a void,
Then fill it with remembered joy.
A friendship shared, a laugh, a kiss...
Ah yes, these things I, too, shall miss.
My life's been full, I've savored much:
Good times, good friends, a loved-one's touch.
Perhaps my time seemed all too brief—
Don't shorten yours with undue grief.
Be not burdened with tears of sorrow,
Enjoy the sunshine of the morrow.

Glasnevin
Cemetery

In Time of Sorrow...

May you see God's light on the path ahead
When the road you walk is dark.
May you always hear,
Even in your hour of sorrow,
The gentle singing of the lark.
When times are hard may hardness
Never turn your heart to stone,
May you always remember
when the shadows fall—
You do not walk alone.

Connemara

4 BLESSING POEMS

Count Your Blessings

Count your blessings instead of your crosses;
Count your gains instead of your losses.
Count your joys instead of your woes;
Count your friends instead of your foes.
Count your smiles instead of your tears;
Count your courage instead of your fears.
Count your full years instead of your lean;
Count your kind deeds instead of your mean.
Count your health instead of your wealth;
Love your neighbor as much as yourself.

Dunaff Head, Inishowen

May Happiness Fill Your Heart

May flowers always line your path
and sunshine light your day.

May songbirds serenade you
every step along the way.

May a rainbow run beside you
in a sky that's always blue.

And may happiness fill your heart each day
your whole life through.

Giant's Causeway

Always Remember

Always remember to forget
the things that made you sad.
But never forget to remember
the things that made you glad.

Always remember to forget
the friends that proved untrue.
But never forget to remember
those that have stuck by you.

Always remember to forget
the troubles that passed away.
But never forget to remember
the blessings that come each day.

Galway Bay

Wishes

I wish you not a path devoid of clouds,
Nor a life on a bed or roses.
Nor, that you might never need regret,
Nor that you should never feel pain.

No, this is not my wish for you. My wish for you is:
That you might be brave in times of trial
When other's lay crosses upon your shoulders.
When mountains must be climbed and chasms crossed,
When hope scarce shines through.
When every gift God gave you might grow along with you,
And let you give the gift of joy to all who care for you.

That you might always have a friend who is worth that name.
Whom you can trust.
And hope will be, in times of sadness,
Who will defy the storms of life by your side.

One more wish for you:
That in every hour of joy and pain, you may be close to God.
This is my wish for you and those who are close to you.
This is my hope for you, now and forever.

PROVERBS

The Irish are also known for their colorful and insightful proverbs; here are a few from my book ***IRISH PROVERBS - Over 200 Insightful Proverbs in 15 Categories:***

Blow not on dead embers.

You'll never plough a field
by turning it over in your mind.

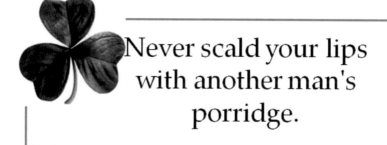

Never scald your lips
with another man's
porridge.

Listen to the sound of the river and you will get a trout.

A nod is as good as a wink to a blind horse.

If you don't want flour on your clothes,
stay out of the mill.

MORE IRISH

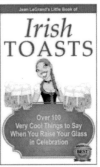

The Irish Heritage Series from Best-Selling Author Jean LeGrand
Available from amazon.com and other book retailers

B⊙ΠUS

Here is a recipe for "Irish Cream Cupcakes" from my book *IRISH TREATS - 30 Dessert Recipes for St. Patrick's Day or Whenever You Want to Celebrate Like the Irish*.

Irish Cream Cupcakes

These cupcakes get rave reviews from everybody who tries 'em ... I'm sure you and your family and friends will enjoy them, too.

24 servings

Total Time: 45 minutes
Prep Time: 25 minutes
Cook Time: 20 minutes + cooling

Ingredients:

½ cup butter, softened
1½ cups granulated white sugar
2 eggs
¾ cup unsweetened applesauce
2 tsp vanilla extract
2½ cups all-purpose flour
3 tsp baking powder
½ tsp salt
½ cup Irish cream liqueur

Frosting:
⅓ cup butter, softened
4 ounces cream cheese (reduced-fat OK)
6 Tbs Irish cream liqueur
4 cups confectioners' sugar

Instructions:

1. Preheat oven to 350°F
2. Put pleated paper cupcake cups into two 12-cup muffin tins
3. In a medium bowl, sift together the flour, baking powder and salt, set aside
4. In a large bowl, beat butter and sugar until crumbly (about 2 minutes)
5. One at a time, add the eggs; beat well after each egg
6. Beat in applesauce and vanilla (mixture may appear curdled)

7. Gradually add the flour/baking soda/salt mixture and liqueur to the creamed mixture (butter, sugar, eggs); mix thoroughly ... alternate between adding the flour/baking soda/salt mixture and the liqueur, beating well after each addition

8. Fill paper-lined muffin cups two-thirds full

9. Bake at 350° for 18-22 minutes. Test for doneness: insert a toothpick near the center, if it comes out clean, the cake is ready

10. Cool for 10 minutes before removing from pans to wire racks to cool completely.

11. In a large mixing bowl, beat butter and cream cheese until fluffy

12. Beat liqueur into the butter/cream cheese mixture

13. Add confectioners' sugar to the butter/cream cheese/liqueur and beat until smooth

14. Spread or pipe the frosting over tops of thoroughly cooled cupcakes

These cupcakes are delicious, and you'll find 29 more great recipes in *Irish Treats* including:

> Desserts using Irish whiskey like: *Irish Whiskey Spice Cake* and *Irish Coffee Pie*

> Desserts using Irish stout like: *Classic Guinness Cake* and *Stout Floats*

> Fruit Dessert like: *Kerry Apple Tart* and *Apple Barley Pudding*

> Cookie & Cookie Bar Desserts like: *Blarney Stones* and *Triple Layer Irish Mint Brownies*

Candy Recipes like: *Yellowman Sponge Toffee* and *Irish Potatoes Candy*

Chocolate Desserts like: *Chocolate Meringue Bread Pudding* and *Chocolate Guinness Cake*

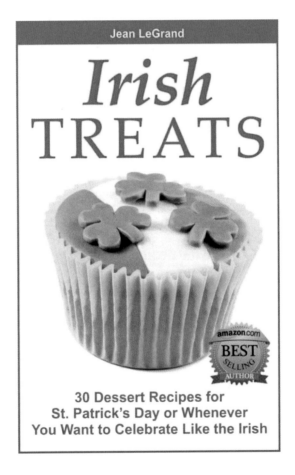

Available from Amazon.com and other retailers.

Can I Ask a Favor?

Thank you so much for reading my book. I hope you really liked it.

As you probably know, many people look at the reviews on line before they decide to purchase a book.

If you liked this book, could you **please take a minute to leave a review** with your feedback?

Just go to the site where you purchased this book, look up *Irish Blessings - Jean LeGrand*, go to the book's page, then scroll down until you see the "Write a customer review button", click it and write a few words about why you like the book.

 A couple of minutes is all I'm asking for, and it would mean the world to me.

Thank you so much,

Jean

PHOTO CREDITS

Introduction Claddagh 2 2008-02-06 (first version); 2008-02-06 (last version) Transferred from **it.wikipedia** Original uploader was **Elyhappy** at **it.wikipedia** This file is licensed under the **Creative Commons Attribution 3.0 Unported** license.

61 Irish Blessings Cliffs of **Slieve League, County Donegal, Ireland** 19 June 2002 Source**http://pdphoto.org/PictureDetail.php?mat=&pg=5942** Author**Jon Sullivan http://pdphoto.org/Copyright.php** This image from **PD Photo.org** has been **released** into the **public domain** by its author and **copyright** holder, Jon Sullivan.

5 St. Patrick's Day Blessings St. Benin's Church, Kilbennan, County Galway, Ireland Detail of stained glass window depicting St. Patrick. September 2010 Self-photographed **Andreas F. Borchert** Reference2010/9735 This file is licensed under the **Creative Commons Attribution-Share Alike 3.0 Germany** license.

28 One Line Blessings Country road in Connemara Winding its way through rocky outcrops with scattered cottages. Aughrusbeg Lough is just off picture to the right. © Copyright **Oliver Dixon** and licensed for reuse under this **Creative Commons Licence**

8 Blessings in Gaelic Geroid Island, Lough Gur According to legend, the goddess Aine, like the Breton Morgan, may sometimes be seen combing her hair, only half her body appearing above the lake. And in times of calmness and clear water, according to another legend, one may behold beneath Aine's lake the lost enchanted castle of her son Geroid, close to Garrod Island—so named from Gerdid or Gerald 27 May 2007 From **geograph.org.uk** **Diarmuid** This file is licensed under the **Creative Commons Attribution-Share Alike 2.0 Generic** license.

A Wedding Blessing Celtic wedding rings **anthony kelly** apdk **January 2, 2009 Canon EOS 30D** This file is licensed under the **Creative Commons Attribution-Share Alike 2.0 Generic** license.

5 Christmas Blessings Doneraile Park and House,Co. Cork Irl. **Liam Moloney** Liamfm **July 3, 2011 Canon EOS Digital Rebel Xsi** This file is licensed under the **Creative Commons Attribution-Share Alike 2.0 Generic** license.

An Easter Blessing Sheep near Roosky Looking north-west from Camcosy Road © Copyright **Kenneth Allen** and licensed for reuse under this **Creative Commons Licence**

2 Funeral Blessings Historic Ireland - Glasnevin Cemetery Is a Hidden Gem And Well Worth a Visit **William Murphy** infomatique **March 19, 2011 Sony NEX-5** This file is licensed under the **Creative Commons Attribution-Share Alike 2.0 Generic** license.

Count Your Blessings Dunaff Head, Inishowen, Co. Dunaff Head in the background with Dunaff and Dunaff Bay, and the street up to the viewpoint at Urrismenagh on the road to Mamore Gap and the Urris Hills. © Copyright **Corinna Schleiffer** and licensed for reuse under this **Creative Commons Licence**

May Happiness Fill Your Heart Giant's Causeway **Anosmia** on **Flickr** May 12, 2012 This file is licensed under the **Creative Commons Attribution 2.0 Generic** license.

Always Remember Ireland Galway-Bay **Michael Bertulat** M. Bertulat **August 26, 2007** This file is licensed under the **Creative Commons Attribution 2.0 Generic** license.

Wishes Connemara **Olivier Bruchez** Olivier Bruchez **August 8, 2011 Screeb, Galway, IE   Casio EX-Z1080** This file is licensed under the **Creative Commons Attribution-Share Alike 2.0 Generic** license.

ஐ AN IRISH TOAST ☙

Here's to women of the Irish shore;
I love but one, I love not more.
But since she's not here to
drink her part,
I'll drink her share with all my heart.

This toast is just one of over 100 found in Jean LeGrand's book: *Irish Toasts*

www.FastForwardPublishing.com

Made in the USA
Las Vegas, NV
07 January 2025

15981058R00040